YORK N(

General Editors: Pro
of Stirling) & Profes
University of Beirut)

Arnold Bennett

THE CARD

Notes by G. D. Killam

Professor of English
University of Guelph

LONGMAN
YORK PRESS

YORK PRESS
Immeuble Esseily, Place Riad Solh, Beirut.

LONGMAN GROUP UK LIMITED
Longman House, Burnt Mill,
Harlow, Essex CM20 2JE, England

First published in 1991

ISBN 0-582-02092-1

Produced by Longman Group (FE) Ltd
Typeset by Gem Graphics, Trenance, Mawgan Porth, Cornwall
Printed in Hong Kong

Contents

Part 1

Introduction

The life of Arnold Bennett

Arnold Bennett was born on 27 May 1867, at Shelton, Hanley, one of the six Staffordshire towns which were later federated into Stoke-on-Trent. He was the eldest of nine children, six of whom survived to adulthood. His father Enoch had followed his own father's trade and become a potter, leaving school at the age of twelve. He returned to school briefly as an apprentice pupil teacher, but was enticed back to the potteries as a partner in a firm that failed. He then kept a pawnshop. He was a man of great ambition, however, and eventually articled himself to a solicitor when he was twenty-nine. Through determined study at night he became a solicitor himself at the age of thirty-four. He was a puritanical Wesleyan Methodist whose domineering temperament left a lasting impression on his children. Bennett was later to evoke this complex father–son relationship in his autobiographical novel *Clayhanger* (1910).

Bennett left Middle School, Newcastle-under-Lyme, at the age of sixteen and with reluctance entered his father's law office. He had literary ambitions, however, and continued his studies at night classes, passing the entrance examinations for London University in 1885. He then sat his legal examinations twice, but failed on both occasions, and in 1888 he determined to leave home. He had already begun a career as a journalist by writing weekly columns for two Staffordshire newspapers. Although his work for his examinations and in his father's law office had not allowed him much recreational time, he had managed to read widely in the works of the English writers of the day. In addition, he had taught himself to read French in order to gain a better knowledge of the contemporary French authors who impressed him. Most importantly, from an employer's point of view, he had learned shorthand, using the Pitman method, a skill quite rare for the time. So, when Bennett came to London in 1888, he had several useful skills and interests, and he succeeded in securing employment with a solicitor's firm in Lincoln's Inn Fields. With this security, he was at last able to develop his enthusiasm for books and music unhindered, and to make contact with writers. He added to his income by collecting and selling old and rare books by mail order, and he began to send short stories to London periodicals.

In 1893 he gave up the law and became assistant editor of the magazine *Woman* and, in 1896, its editor. He wrote book reviews and short stories; and as 'Marjorie' he wrote a gossip column and answered 'letters' sent to the editor. Through this experience Bennett learned the craft of the newspaper trade and was able to pursue a lifelong career in journalism. Moreover, he came to have an intimate understanding of the concerns of women in his society and was able to draw upon this understanding when later he came to write his novels. Bennett was recognised in his day – and is still thought of – as one of the most sympathetic male novelists to write about the nature and quality of women's lives.

In 1894 the *Yellow Book*, a new and highly fashionable periodical edited by Aubrey Beardsley and Henry Harland, published his short story 'A Letter Home', which was well received and announced his 'arrival' on the literary scene. In the same year he began work on his first sustained piece of fiction, the novel *A Man from the North*. Published in 1898, it presents a realistic picture of the attempts of a young man from the Potteries to come to terms with London life as an office clerk. The events of the novel were obviously in part inspired by Bennett's early experiences in London, but they were also strongly influenced by *A Mummer's Wife*, written by his Irish contemporary George Moore in 1884. These two strands of inspiration – personal experience and literary stimulus – were to mark Bennett's future work. He was also to write an astonishing range of literature: serious fiction, light fiction and journalism coincidentally, seeing no paradox in these apparently disparate kinds of activity.

In 1900 he gave up the editorship of *Woman* in order to devote himself to a full-time career as a writer. His second novel, *The Grand Babylon Hotel* (1902), is a light-hearted popular work of a kind Bennett was to write throughout his life (*The Card* is a typical example) and reveals Bennett's fascination with sumptuous living, a life-style he was progressively to cultivate as his fortunes grew. Bennett established his reputation as a serious novelist with *Anna of the Five Towns* in 1902, in which he draws on his youthful experience of the Potteries of Staffordshire and exposes 'the great and powerful class of house-tyrants, the backbone of the British nation', their materialism and the narrowness of their lives, personified in the wealthy but miserly father of Anna Tellwright. Anna chooses familial loyalty over personal happiness and freedom, another theme to which Bennett would return in later novels.

In 1902, attracted by the French literary scene and the realist and naturalist writers of the period – Zola, Flaubert, Maupassant and the brothers de Goncourt – Bennett went to France. Before leaving England, however, he wrote anonymously an autobiographical work,

The Truth about an Author (1903). Meant to be taken as a light-hearted and satirical entertainment which debunked literary pomposity and pretentiousness, it was instead received as a serious autobiography which suggested that the author's overriding concern in his literary works was to gain financially from their publication. This misunderstanding was to haunt Bennett throughout his life.

Bennett remained in France for nearly ten years, making only intermittent trips to England. He contributed articles to various English periodicals and newspapers and, after an initial lonely period, became a part of French literary society. In doing so, he made the acquaintance of several of those authors whose works had attracted him in England. It was here that he married Marguerite Soulié in 1907 and wrote the first of his several masterpieces, *The Old Wives' Tale*, published in 1908. In this book, Bennett elaborates the theme he explored in *Anna of the Five Towns* and tells the story of the contrasting lives of two sisters, Sophia and Constance. The characters of the sisters and of those around them are drawn with great compassion. Constance (as her name suggests) chooses to stay at home in her father's draper's shop, and eventually marries the shop's chief assistant, Samuel Povey. Sophia elopes with the attractive Gerald Scales to Paris, but is deserted and has to struggle to survive. The two sisters are eventually reunited, and live out their old age reflecting on the past in the town where they were born.

The first of the 'Clayhanger novels', *Clayhanger*, was published in 1910. Here, Bennett once again returns to the Potteries to tell the story of Edwin Clayhanger and his relationship with his repressive father, Darius. It is his ability to invest the ordinariness of Edwin's life with emotional intensity wrought from the powerful recollection of his own early years in the drab and forbidding Midlands, an ability enhanced by the influence of the French realists on his fictional craft, that account for Bennett being called by one of his contemporaries 'a connoisseur of the normal'. *Hilda Lessways* (1911) and *These Twain* (1916) complete the Clayhanger trilogy.

By 1911 Bennett was a successful man of letters. His popularity was secure in England and confirmed in the United States where the success of *The Old Wives' Tale* had assured him a lucrative publishing deal, and where he made a six week trip, visiting six major American cities, in all of which he was acclaimed.

In 1918, towards the end of the First World War, he served as Director of Propaganda for the Ministry of Information. His opinions on political matters associated with the war were sought and valued. He became the close friend of Lord Beaverbrook, who at the time was head of the Ministry of Information and later became a hugely successful newspaper proprietor. This friendship endured throughout

Bennett's life. In a series of political articles on various topics written for the *Daily News*, which ran throughout the war, he pointed out inefficiencies in the conduct of the war, looking in particular at the ill-treatment of soldiers and their families by the government, and the spread of misleading information with regard to recruitment campaigns. He attacked the jingoism of certain of the popular newspapers and the supporters of conscription, and he was active in fundraising campaigns.

All this time he continued to write fiction and to enjoy modest success as a playwright. Bennett's last two major novels are *Riceyman Steps* (1923) and *Lord Raingo* (1926), the former written in a familiar Bennett manner, the latter a departure in subject matter from all of his other serious writing. *Riceyman Steps* is the story of Henry Earlforward, an East London bookseller, who, in middle age, marries Violet Arb, a widow. Bennett shows how the two contrasting temperaments in Earlforward, a lifetime of miserliness which makes domestic contentment impossible and an ingrained gentleness which makes rebellion unthinkable, destroy any potential the couple have for happiness. Here again Bennett invests a homely and ordinary situation with tragic intensity. The novel was both a popular and a critical success, and Thomas Hardy, Joseph Conrad and H. G. Wells praised it highly. In complete contrast *Lord Raingo* derives its central themes from Bennett's experience of public service during the First World War. The novel tells of the rise to and fall from power of Sam Raingo, a self-made millionaire. Against the background of Raingo's quest for a peerage, the contrast between his strained relationship with his snobbish, self-indulgent wife, Adela, and his genuine love for an ordinary girl, Delphine, is revealed. Moreover, because of his experience of government workings, Bennett is able to reveal with great skill his understanding of ministerial in-fighting, inter-cabinet intrigue at all levels of a wartime government and the menace and corruption of power.

Altogether Bennett wrote and published eighty-four books, almost evenly divided between novels, short stories, plays and journalistic pieces. Considering how prolific Bennett was in all his various guises, there is a remarkable consensus amongst critics as to his best work. Of the novels mentioned above, three could justifiably claim to be of the highest standard – *The Old Wives' Tale*, *Clayhanger* and *Riceyman Steps*. The others are all considerable works with their own merits, but not quite in the class of these three. This is not to say that his less serious fiction – of which *The Card* is one of the most durable pieces – is less rewarding or of less value. It was well received in its day, in the United States as well as in England, and was as much a factor in creating his substantial wealth as were the major works. He enjoyed success on the London stage as well (though never as much as he hoped for), and as his career flourished he became a major force in literary journalism, as generous in praising new talent when he discovered it – Aldous Huxley, D. H. Lawrence, James Joyce and many others – as he was with his peers, who numbered among them over the years some of the most famous names in modern English literature – Henry James, Thomas Hardy, George Moore, Joseph Conrad, Rudyard Kipling, H. G. Wells, John Galsworthy, Ford Madox Ford and E. M. Forster.

Bennett was maligned by some of his contemporaries for what they regarded as a lack of sensitivity. Most notable – or perhaps enduring – was the satire by Ezra Pound in the 'Mr Nixon' stanzas in *Hugh Selwyn Mauberley* (1920). Bennett was a very astute businessman and realised that he had to keep up a steady 'production line' of work if he was going to be able to make a comfortable living from his writing. This attitude offended some of the younger writers in his later years, particularly figures such as Pound, Wyndham Lewis and Lawrence, who held that capitalism and literary achievement could not exist simultaneously. This was not Bennett's view, and he succeeded in proving them wrong in his best novels, but the main thrust of his artistic outlook came from the fact that he was a very practical man who had no time for pretentiousness and agonised aesthetic considerations. He became a rich man from his writing and had no fear of the lampooning he would get for flaunting this wealth. There is no doubt that his compulsion always to be writing produced work of low quality, but at the same time, the best of his books stand comparison with many of the best works of those who were quick to criticise him.

Bennett's personal life was plagued by an acute stammer which left him shy and lacking in social confidence, especially when talking to women. His marriage to Marguerite dragged on until 1920, and it was not until 1922 that he found the happiness he had been looking for, when he formed a permanent liaison with Dorothy Cheston, an actress with her own successful career. They had a daughter, and Dorothy took Bennett's name by deed poll.

Bennett always feared that he might suffer a slow, lingering death. This was the fate his father had met – he died at the age of fifty-eight – and it is, significantly, also the fate of two of his fictional characters. Darius Clayhanger's slow decline is depicted in a grimly convincing way, and Sam Raingo succumbs to a degenerative heart disease only after a long period of suffering. Bennett mentioned his fear of such a death on more than one occasion to Dorothy, and in the event his fear proved well founded. He contracted typhoid fever from the tap water during a trip to Paris and died on 26 March 1931 after a lengthy, debilitating illness. There is no clear evidence to show that he drank the tainted water in a deliberate attempt to do himself harm, but this theory still remains a mysterious possibility.

Bennett's reputation and *The Card*

While, as discussed above, Bennett's reputation rests principally on three novels – *The Old Wives' Tale*, *Clayhanger* and *Riceyman Steps* – his less serious, light-hearted novels like *The Card* deserve attention. They were very popular with a large number of intelligent readers in their day, as well as with the less-educated reading public, because of their genuine humour and high spirits. More than one critic has noted that in making a strict division between the serious novels – *The Old Wives' Tale*, *Clayhanger* and *Riceyman Steps* – and the lighter works – *The Card* and its sequel *The Regent* and books such as *Buried Alive* and *Mr Prohack* – it is difficult for the student to realise the full range of Bennett's talent. Novels such as *The Card* reveal an alternative side to his artistry. In his serious work he displays an understanding of emotion and situation on a deep psychological level, but it is in his so-called light novels that he displays his understanding of the hopes and dreams of ordinary people. It is this understanding that made his lighter novels so popular with the general, and often not highly educated, reading public of his time. These novels could justifiably be described as romances or escapist entertainments, but they are constructed with more skill and care than the run-of-the-mill examples of the genre. Bennett presents a number of remarkable characters in remarkable situations, but in each case they are given a sufficiently compelling human touch to make them believable and acceptable to his audience.

The Card is an outstanding example of Bennett's lighter work, and indeed until very recently the general and critical impression of the book was of a work of escapism designed to entertain its readers. Critics in the past few years, however, have drawn attention to a darker side to Denry's story and have remarked that Bennett, in displaying Denry's quest to be 'truly magnificent', his amassing of considerable wealth through 'honest ingenuity', ignored the inevitable ruthlessness which accompanies his determination to succeed and the pain that this must inevitably have caused those who stood in his way. We get some hint of this in his responses to Councillor Cotterill when he becomes bankrupt. The critic John Lucas writes that the characteristic tone of the novel '. . . is an attempt to deflect unsympathetic responses to Denry' and that the final lines of the novel – 'He's identified . . . with the great cause of cheering us all up' – is the most blatant example of this kind of deflection.

There would seem to be no doubt that had Bennett attempted a full exploration of the implications of Denry's methods of self-advancement, had he matched boldness with ruthlessness, cheerfulness with cynicism, a different kind of novel would have resulted, one more closely in tune with the satire and sarcasm implicit in some of the greatest novels written in a similar episodic style to *The Card*.

The background to *The Card*

The setting of *The Card* is the Potteries region of Bennett's own birth and early years. Named Bursley in the novel, one of the 'Five Towns' which were to form the locales of many of Bennett's early fictions, it resembles Hanley where Bennett was born. (There were in fact six towns but Bennett adopted some poetic licence here. They now make up the city of Stoke-on-Trent.) The Potteries were one of the earliest industrial developments in England and represented for many writers – notable among them Disraeli, Mrs Gaskell and Dickens – both a new kind of power based on the accumulation of wealth by the few, and its effect, a heretofore unknown kind of poverty, both social and spiritual among the many, the working classes. This development was regarded with fear and disgust by these writers, and their fiction exposes and attacks the immorality and injustice which these conditions bred.

In contrast to the apocalyptic vision of Dickens in *Hard Times* (1854), Bennett did not see the Potteries as strange and threatening, but as familiar home territory. He recognised their ugliness and the drab lives of the majority of their inhabitants, but he knew that if he was to fulfil his wish to embellish his novels and keep them true to life, he would have to make the best of the materials at hand. In doing so, he drew heavily on the French writers, primarily of the 1870s and 1880s, who are grouped under the umbrella term 'naturalists'. These writers – Zola, Flaubert, Maupassant and the brothers Edmond and Jules de Goncourt – attempted to show in several experimental novels that beauty was more a matter of the perspective from which a subject was viewed than something inherent in the subject. In their novels, particularly those of Zola, such as *Thérèse Raquin* (1868) and *Germinal* (1885), man is seen as an element of the novel, of no more or less significance than any other element, and subject to the power of the natural forces around him. Bennett was most influenced by the aspect of naturalism that emphasised the primacy of everyday life as opposed to intellectual aspirations. He attempts to transform the drab and the trivial in Potteries life into something exciting and adventurous. Instead of transporting his readers to distant or imagined fantasy places, he uses the stuff of their own lives and brings out their positive qualities. *The Card* is a typical example of this method, for no matter how extraordinary Denry's achievements become, he never leaves home for long and he is always clearly identified as a part of Bursley life.

In following the example of the French naturalists in his writing rather than the English novelists of Dickens's generation, Bennett discovered fresh possibilities for his craft. In his most serious novels, this influence allowed him to recognise and celebrate the continuities of everyday existence – the consolations in the balance between ageing and constancy – the continuities which reside below life's surface but have such a powerful influence over an individual's action or inaction. In this sense Bennett's novels are warmer, more sympathetic than the writing of his French mentors, and because of this they achieve what one critic has called a 'limited universality'.

Although Bennett left the Five Towns when still a young man, he was to draw on their atmosphere and history for a good deal of his life as a writer. Recognising the region's lack of obvious beauty and his own deeper wish to describe and celebrate the beautiful, knowing that the harsh puritanism inherent in the Methodism practised by his father provided a necessary but cold consolation for the ugliness of people's surroundings, Bennett left for the distant scene of London, in every way bigger than the Potteries, which he supposed would offer him the chance to satisfy his creative desires. Away from the Five Towns he found the freedom he needed to give full and free expression to his spiritual concerns. He was never to return to the Potteries as anything other than an occasional visitor, yet they had made such a significant impression on his consciousness that he was continually to resurrect them as the setting for his novels. The fact that some of these novels are regarded as minor classics of modern fiction is striking testament to the powerful and vivid influence Bennett's early life had on his writing, and of the success with which he displayed this influence in his work.

Bennett's view of life is not tragic: rather it is one of stoical acceptance of things as they are. In *The Card*, however, he creates in Denry a character who does not accept what his surroundings have to offer but rather exploits them for the purposes of making a full and exciting life for himself. Denry is the person Bennett could not be, a fantasy, all-powerful figure – it is interesting to note that Bennett gives Denry his own birthdate. Denry can and does remain in the Five Towns and triumphs over their meanness, pettiness and grinding ugliness. In fact, Denry so transcends the dull and banal in everyday Bursley that he is unaware that these negative aspects exist.

A note on the text

The Card: A Story of Adventure in the Five Towns was begun on 3 January 1909 and finished on 1 March. Bennett tells us in his journals that he had the story of Denry in mind as early as November 1908 and that it was to be 'purely humorous and light, but . . . true to life'. He plotted the story in twelve five-thousand-word chapters, each a single adventure of Denry's but each fitting into a continuous narrative. Bennett also planned that the novel would have serial publication, as its form indicates. The title for the serial was to be *Denry, the Audacious*. To protect American copyright three chapters were published by Dutton in New York as *The Deeds of Denry the Audacious*. The novel was hugely successful, going through forty editions from 1911 to 1964 with the publishers Methuen. It has also been adapted for the stage as a play and a musical comedy, and was successfully made into a film in 1951 with Alec Guinness as Denry. It is widely available in a Penguin edition, first published as a Penguin Modern Classic in 1975, reissued as a Penguin Twentieth Century Classic in 1991.

Part 2

Summaries
of THE CARD

A general summary

The Card is the story of a man from the working classes in the Potteries' town of Bursley in the Midlands of England and of his rise to become the town's most prominent official, its Mayor. As a young man he sees early in life that success is achieved more by audacity than learning, and more by chance happenings than design. The Card – Edward Machin (known as Denry) – is quick to recognise the opportunities for self-advancement that chance provides, and he is bold in seizing them.

Denry is born in Bursley, the most ancient of the Five Towns, in 1867. (As we have noted, Bennett gave Denry his own birthday, thus making apparent the autobiographical element in the novel.) As a young student Denry is neither intellectual nor industrious, but he is audacious from the start. By altering the grade received in a geography test, placing a '2' in front of the '7' he had scored out of '30', he wins a scholarship to a Board School and receives a better than average education.

When he leaves school, Denry joins the law offices of Mr Duncalf who is also the Town Clerk of Bursley. He is entrusted with issuing invitations to a municipal ball to be given by the rich, young and pretty Countess of Chell. He boldly gives himself an invitation to this select occasion and becomes a celebrity at the ball when he asks the Countess to dance, has his invitation accepted and causes the Countess to laugh at a chance remark. He becomes the envy of Bursley society, especially when it is learned that the Countess has refused other invitations to dance. His reputation rises further when he and the Countess exchange remarks as she and her husband, the Earl of Chell and Mayor of Bursley, leave the ball. Denry realises that through his audacity and luck he has become 'The envied of all' and someone to be reckoned with in Bursley society.

Denry is sacked by Mr Duncalf for abusing the trust placed in him by giving himself an invitation to the ball. He opens his own business as a rent collector and estate agent, and he makes loans, for which he charges a modest rate of interest, to tenants who are behind in their rents. Thus Denry begins to achieve the wealth that will pave the way to creating the 'magnificence' he desires as a result of his success at the ball. Such is his success that he gains the most admired reputation in his society, that of being 'a card'; and such is the audacity of his ventures that he becomes known not simply as *a* card but as *the* card. Despite his success in business, however, Denry knows that he will have to earn much more money if he is to accomplish his desire to be truly magnificent. While he is considering his future he becomes more involved with Ruth Earp, a girl who had given him dancing lessons in exchange for an illegal invitation to the Countess's ball. He saves her from the embarrassment of being in arrears with her rent and for a brief time is engaged to be married to her. But on a holiday trip to Llandudno in Wales he realises that she is more interested in his money than in himself, and the engagement comes to an end.

This does not mean that Denry's trip to Llandudno is a total waste of time, for it is here that Denry increases his reputation in Bursley and has his first financial breakthrough. He writes a special report for the Potteries' newspaper, *The Staffordshire Signal*, about the ship-wreck of a Norwegian barque in a terrible summer storm. In his report, he draws on his recollections of the rescue attempt in which he participated and Ruth witnessed, and which had led him to discover Ruth's extravagance as she spent all of his money on bags of chocolate for the shipwrecked sailors. Recognising that well-to-do holidaymakers will spend money readily for diversions, he buys the lifeboat that was used to rescue the Norwegian vessel and converts it into a touring craft to take the inquisitive to see the wrecked ship at first hand. He also arranges to have a photographer take pictures of the tourists in the lifeboat and takes a percentage in commission from each customer. He markets a lemon-flavoured chocolate bar as a seasickness remedy, from which he makes further profit and an outright sum of £200 when he sells the rights to produce the concoction to a local manufacturer. All of these schemes help Denry to establish the basis of his future fortune. When he arrives home in Bursley with a hatbox full of sovereigns for his mother, his position as a 'card' is consolidated.

Back in Bursley, Denry founds the Universal Thrift Club, a kind of credit union, and seeks the patronage of the Countess of Chell in launching it. He is inadvertently locked in Sneyd Hall, the residence of the Countess, and in his attempt to find a way out he becomes intimately acquainted with the ancestral stately home and its decoration. When the maid of the Countess finally re-opens the doors in the Hall, Denry makes good his escape. The startled maid is quoted in *The Signal* as having seen off 'a burglar of Herculean physique and Titanic proportions'. The identity of the mystery burglar is keenly sought, but Denry avoids discovery because of the maid's incompetence. When he describes the splendour of the residence in one of his occasional articles for *The Signal*, he conveys the impression, without making a claim, that his intimacy with the Countess has been maintained, while skilfully avoiding discovery as the 'burglar'.

On this occasion, Denry's reputation as an intimate friend of the Countess has been enhanced by pretence, since he did not, in fact, meet her to discuss the Universal Thrift Club. Events, however, conspire to make his actual meeting with the Countess a matter of the most pressing concern. The Universal Thrift Club has been more successful than Denry imagined and, in urgent need of capital, determined to achieve the patronage of the Countess, he conspires with her driver to effect the breakdown of her carriage on the way to an important public engagement. In a journey filled with adventure, Denry gets the Countess to her meeting on time, finds himself on the platform with distinguished public figures, and seconds the vote of thanks to the Countess. The Countess, indebted to Denry, becomes the patroness of the Thrift Club, and this vote of confidence in the Club ensures its survival and thus secures Denry's financial position.

Such is Denry's financial security that he can indulge in a complicated scheme to remove his mother from the tiny and uncomfortable cottage in which they both live. By telling her that he acts as the agent for a rich Londoner (a former Bursleyan) who is building a fine new house with the intention of returning to the Five Towns, and by convincing her that her own cottage has been bought up by this man and is due for destruction, Denry is able to show his mother the new house and hear her admit that it is the most sensible kind of house she has ever seen, before confessing that it is, in fact, his house and her new home.

With this matter settled, Denry decides to enter the newspaper business, in search of new avenues of experience. He invests in a venture which involves the transformation of a weekly newspaper, the *Five Towns Weekly*, into a daily paper, the *Five Towns Daily*. The new paper enters into a tortuous rivalry with the established daily newspaper of the Five Towns, *The Signal*. *The Signal* employs bullying tactics to sabotage the newsboys for the *Daily* and, on the day of a crucial football match, lures them with toasted cheese and hot tarts into a warehouse where they are confined.

It appears that for once Denry has been defeated. But he turns the tables on *The Signal* by commandeering circus wagons which have been hired by *The Signal* for its thirty-fifth anniversary celebrations. He buys all the copies of *The Signal* and uses the wagons as kiosks to sell copies of the *Daily*. He then uses copies of *The Signal* to wrap up packets of Turkish Delight won by contestants in a new kind of coconut shy, 'knock the signal down'. In this way, 'the card' wins again.

Councillor Cotterill, a property developer and father of Ruth Earp's friend Nellie, whom Denry had encountered in Llandudno, finds himself in severe financial difficulties. Through bad management he is forced to file for bankruptcy and to set off for Toronto in Canada to attempt a fresh start. Denry, with Ruth Earp (who has recently returned to Bursley as a widow, after the death of her wealthy husband, a Mr Capron-Smith), travel to Liverpool to take Cotterill, his wife and Nellie out of steerage, the lowliest class of steamship accommodation, and relocate them in second class. On a typical impulse, Denry deserts Ruth and whisks Nellie away, suddenly intent on marrying her.

The marriage does indeed take place, and Denry and Nellie spend their honeymoon at the Hôtel Beau-Site in Mont Pridoux, Switzerland. There they meet a number of holidaymakers, predominantly British, enjoy their first exposure to the winter sports of lugeing (a one-person toboggan) and skiing. Denry takes the opportunity to expose the excessive snobbery of a Captain Deverax who has insulted him.

Denry finally reaches the summit of his ambition, to become the youngest Mayor in the history of Bursley. He achieves this by saving the Bursley Football Club from extinction by arranging to have England's most distinguished football player – and a native of Bursley – join the club.

Detailed summaries

Chapter 1

The Card is the story of the rise of a young man from the working classes in the Potteries of the Midlands of England to become the town's most prominent official, its Mayor. Edward Henry Machin – called Denry for short – learns early in his life that success is achieved more by audacity than learning, more by chance than design. He is neither intellectual nor industrious, but rather survives on his flair and bravado. The first example of this daring is when he alters the grade he achieves in a geography test. He arrives early for an examination, finds the classroom empty and sees that the result he has achieved in the geography test is 7 marks out of a possible 30. He boldly places a '2' in front of the '7', thus altering the grade to '27', leaves the room and returns late for the examination, to avoid any suspicion or the discovery of his cheating. Through this act of daring and deceit he wins a scholarship to a Board School which provides a better than average education. His achievement at the Board School is undistinguished, but it qualifies him, when he leaves, to join the law offices of Mr Duncalf, who is also the Town Clerk of Bursley.

Denry works mainly as a rent collector for Mr Duncalf, but he is entrusted with the task of issuing invitations to a municipal ball to be given by the rich, young and pretty Countess of Chell. He decides that he will attend the ball, even though he is not one of the privileged members of Bursley society who have been invited. He issues an invitation to himself, and when he realises he needs a dress suit, he arranges for a tailor to make it for him in return for generous terms of credit regarding repayment and a ticket to the ball. He issues another undeserved invitation to Miss Ruth Earp in exchange for dancing lessons. On the evening of the ball, Denry becomes something of a local celebrity when, in response to a bet from Harold Etches, a wealthy young manufacturer, he asks the Countess to dance, in front of all the distinguished guests, including his employer Mr Duncalf. The Countess accepts, and Denry makes her laugh with his quick, cheeky response to her polite questions. He is not at all certain what he has said to provoke her laughter, but he is quick to recognise that it has made him the envy of others at the ball. Through this act of daring, Denry is further convinced of the value of action and accepts the £5 bet from Harold Etches with an air of nonchalance. He thus has his first success in Bursley society, which is enhanced when it is learned that the Countess has refused other invitations to dance. His reputation is even further enhanced when he and the Countess exchange remarks as she and her husband, the Earl of Chell and Mayor of Bursley, leave. Again the Countess laughs at Denry's comments. Again Denry is uncertain what he has said to make the Countess laugh, but he realises that through his audacity and through good luck he has become 'The envied of all' and someone to be reckoned with in Bursley society.

COMMENTARY:
Bennett sets the light-hearted and ironic tone of the novel and announces the quality of daring in his hero when he says that Denry is an 'extraordinary man', born into modest working-class surroundings, and he seeks to make this immediately apparent in the incident when Denry cheats in the geography examination. 'Of course it was dishonest', writes Bennett, but 'Every schoolboy is dishonest', and 'All is fair between schoolboys and schoolmasters.'

NOTES AND GLOSSARY:
potbanks: a factory where earthenware vessels are made

| peer: | the equal of |
| carillons: | in this case, the laughter of the Countess is compared with the melodious pealing of church bells |

Chapter 2

Denry, now drenched in a vast desire to be truly magnificent, is admired and envied as a wonderful and dazzling fellow as a result of his success at the ball. This is not, however, a view shared by his employer, Mr Duncalf, who sacks Denry for issuing invitations to himself, Ruth Earp and his tailor, people who were not on the guest list and therefore not entitled to be present at the Countess's ball. This setback is not a total disaster for Denry because he believes that his life is governed by chance and coincidence and that some great coincidence will soon occur to change the situation for the better. In fact, the coincidence that sets Denry up as a rent collector is very much manufactured by himself. He makes a point of arriving late for church one Sunday, at the same time as the habitually late Mrs Codleyn. She is a property owner, and Denry has collected her rents as part of his duties for Mr Duncalf; but Mrs Codleyn has become dissatisfied with the service Mr Duncalf is providing in managing her rented properties. Unbeknown to Mrs Codleyn, Denry is party to this information, and as a first step in a move to achieve independence and a financial base for himself, he offers to manage her properties for her. He assures her that he will give a better service than that offered by Mr Duncalf: he will render the accounts more frequently than Duncalf and he will charge a lower fee. Mrs Codleyn hires him, so setting him on the path that will lead to his later fortune. He establishes himself in business as a rent collector, estate agent and 'philanthropist' – he makes loans to tenants in arrears with their rents. For this service he charges a modest rate of interest. His fortunes begin to rise, so much so, in fact, that he is invited to join the 'correctly exclusive' Sports Club where only the most socially prominent of Bursley society are members. Denry more and more comes to see himself as a peculiarly gifted young man, a man who is destined for success. He comes to regard himself as the most admired type of person in cities like Bursley – 'a card'. When challenged by a member of the Sports Club about the dubious nature of his business dealings, he responds by giving away a house he has just purchased to an aged and poverty-stricken woman. The gesture is seen by his fellows to be a unique act of generosity, and Denry is now perceived as being not only *a* card but *the* card.

NOTES AND GLOSSARY:

sempstress: a seamstress

card: a celebrity, known for his audacity, his invention, his ability to surprise and delight, to seize an opportunity and turn it to his advantage

dash: showy appearance or display

Chapter 3

As Denry's financial circumstances become secure, he recognises the need to develop the necessary social graces which will allow him to move around in smart Bursley society. He is realistic about his position so far, which does not give him the financial weight to earn social prestige, but he feels that his lack of social refinement is a real drawback. He sets about making amends for this flaw when he becomes re-acquainted with Ruth Earp, his former dancing teacher, who has fallen in arrears with her rent.

Acting on behalf of Mr Herbert Calvert, the owner of the property Ruth Earp rents, Denry calls on her to collect the money that is owing to his client. He is impressed by her refined, moderately luxurious and stylish life, and recognises that this is something he wishes to emulate. Ruth employs various devices to forestall giving Denry the money for the rent. She tells Denry initially that Mr Calvert has paid court to her and made advances to her and thus has waived the payment of her rent. She claims that when she rejected him, he behaved very badly and, in sending Denry to collect the rent, is acting vindictively towards her. She then promises Denry a cheque for the overdue rent if he will call the next day. When he calls, Ruth plies Denry with a splendid tea. In the midst of her sumptuous surroundings Denry realises that he has a long way to go before he will be able to live in comparable style. It is here in this luxurious flat that the idea of marriage to Ruth Earp first occurs to him. When she suddenly feels faint and he is able to assist her, he feels even more tenderly disposed towards her. She then asks Denry to remove the money for the rent from a locked desk drawer. When the lock proves to be broken, she asks Denry to arrange for a locksmith to visit and repair it and asks him to collect the rent money the following morning. He complies with her requests.

As Denry returns from the Sports Club late in the same evening, he sees a driverless pantechnicon van rolling down a street towards the city canal. With foolhardy courage, Denry jumps on to the van and tries to stop its progress. He does not succeed, and the van crashes through the gates of a company yard, ending up in the local canal. Miss Earp is inside, and the brave Denry saves her life. She has planned to leave Bursley at night with all her worldly possessions. She admits that her promises to Denry were meant to delay him until she could escape, and confesses that she has no money. She explains that the van 'got off' while its horses were in stables and its drivers were resting, waiting for night to fall before setting off for Birmingham where Ruth Earp's father lives.

Rather than being angry with her for her deceit and duplicity, Denry recognises in Ruth an audacity equal to his own, and he feels that they are kindred spirits. His compassion aroused by this insight, Denry destroys evidence which will connect Ruth with the incident, is given credit for his attempt to save the van, and pays part of the rent that she owes Mr Calvert from his own funds. In this way, their strange courtship gets underway.

NOTES AND GLOSSARY:

smuts: blackened with smoke and soot from the potteries

pantechnicon van: a large van used for furniture removals. At the time *The Card* was written, it would have been horsedrawn

bloods and blades: young men of good birth with financial independence

Henry Mynors . . . Anna Tellwright . . . Ephraim Tellwright: these are all characters from Bennett's earlier novel, *Anna of the Five Towns* (1902). This sort of reference to characters in other stories is a device which Bennett uses throughout his novels concerning the Five Towns, and it establishes a sense of continuity between these works

coming the duke: behaving in a superior and patronising manner

hook it on the q.t.: run away without being detected

Chapter 4

Denry and Ruth are now engaged to be married. They decide to travel to the Welsh holiday town of Llandudno 'by custom in virtue' – that is to say, in the company of a chaperone, in this case Nellie Cotterill, the girl Denry met with Ruth at the Countess of Chell's ball. Denry has never seen the sea before, and while he is impressed with its beauty, he is more interested in any potential opportunities for amassing wealth by honest ingenuity. There are fifty thousand holidaymakers who seek distractions from their everyday lives, and they are willing to pay handsomely for fresh amusements. Denry sets out to discover how to win a portion of this substantial holiday spending. He also learns on this vacation that

Ruth is a spendthrift. It appears to him that she is interested in him only for his money and that she is very adept at spending it. While Denry is considering how to curb Ruth's furious spending, a fierce storm blows up, and a Norwegian barque, the *Hjalmar*, is wrecked as it heads for the harbour. Denry writes an account of the storm, the wreck and the heroic rescue operation mounted by the coastguard of the port for *The Staffordshire Signal* newspaper – his first journalistic endeavour. When this is published, his reputation in Bursley is further enhanced, as *The Signal* is a local paper. During his participation in the rescue operation, Denry asks Ruth to take care of an amount of money which he carries in his pockets, part of the rents he has been collecting. He fears that if he falls in the sea the weight of the coins will pull him down. When the rescue is accomplished, he returns ashore to find that Ruth has spent all this money on buying chocolate from penny-in-the-slot machines and dispensing it to members of the rescued Norwegian crew. Denry is angered by the irresponsibility of this display of needless benevolence. When Ruth's spendthrift tendencies grow more apparent, Denry makes no offer to pay for her accommodation. In this way, his engagement to Ruth comes to an end.

Denry now becomes preoccupied with a scheme to exploit the wreck of the Norwegian barque for his own profit. As a first step, he arranges to purchase *The Fleetwing*, the ancient Llandudno lifeboat which saved the crew of the wrecked Norwegian barque, from its owner, Cregeen. He sees Ruth and Nellie off at the station and puts Ruth in her place when, in a final act of wasteful greed, she asks Denry to buy her a paperweight at the station kiosk. Denry sarcastically reserves the trinket in the name of 'Rothschild', confirming the breach between them.

NOTES AND GLOSSARY:

char-à-bancs:	motor coaches used for sightseeing tours
bodkin:	an archaic word for a dagger
sang-froid:	coolness; calmness
barque:	a sailing vessel with three or more masts
preprandial:	any activity engaged in before dinner
odd man:	domestic servant at a lodging house
Rothschild:	Denry's engagement to Ruth ends with a single word, 'Rothschild'. In using this one word Denry suggests that Ruth is behaving as if she were as wealthy as the fabulously rich family of bankers named Rothschild

Chapter 5

Denry hires a crew of sailors to man *The Fleetwing* and take holiday-makers out to see the wreck of the *Hjalmar*. Having invested most of his money in the venture, he is fearful that it will fail, but in fact it proves a great success. Denry seems to be surprised that such a simple idea can reap such rewards. As the tours increase in popularity, rival tours are mounted; but Denry's remain the most popular because his boat is the one which effected the rescue of the sailors in distress. He becomes a notable figure in the town, recognised by almost everyone. His reputation increases when he introduces 'Rocket Fêtes' each evening in September as the holiday season draws to a close. Not only has Denry woken the town up, but he has grown moderately rich from the proceeds.

Equally successful is his making and marketing of a lemon-flavoured chocolate bar (a sweet invented by chance by Nellie Cotterill, Ruth's companion) as a cure for seasickness. Eventually he sells the rights to manufacture the chocolate bar to a local business-man for £200.

Denry's third commercial venture in Llandudno is likewise successful. He arranges with a local photographer to take pictures of tourists at the site of the shipwreck, from each of which he receives a commission. This adds further to his profits. Eventually the citizens of Llandudno come to resent his success and the fact that he is taking money out of the town. However, by the time he gives up his tourist business, Denry's fortunes have further risen, as has his reputation for shrewdness. He is able to end his summer business ventures by giving an elaborate dinner in the most expensive hotel in the city to Nellie Cotterill and her parents, Councillor Cotterill and his wife, who visit Llandudno at the close of the season. The Councillor is a property developer in his forties, who treats Denry as an inferior and calls him 'young man'. While he resents Councillor Cotterill's patronising attitude towards him, Denry knows he has made an impression as an up-and-coming fellow. He returns to Bursley a happy and successful man – with a hatbox full of sovereigns for his mother.

COMMENTARY:

Note how often Bennett includes three episodes in each of the chapters of the book. Here, the creation of the boat trip for tourists, the lemon-flavoured chocolate for them to eat as they tour, and the photographs that are taken as a record of their holiday lend unity to the chapter.

Chapter 6

Denry now thinks of himself as the premier card in Bursley, 'the very ace of the town', and adds further to his reputation for eccentric behaviour by buying a mule and a victoria carriage – 'funny without being vulgar' and a more effective advertising tool than a sandwich-man. Not only is the carriage an ingenious method of publicity, but Denry is intent that this eccentric purchase should further embellish his position as the town's leading 'card' and 'character', making sure that any challengers are put firmly in their place. He also acquires an office and office-boy to cope with his growing business success, which reaches new heights when he founds the Universal Thrift Club.

The Club acts as a kind of bank or credit union into which Denry takes money from interested parties for safe-keeping, issues them with Thrift Club tickets, and arranges for local businesses to accept the tickets as payment for goods received, tickets which Denry then redeems for cash. He secures the success of this venture by allowing members of the Thrift Club to purchase goods to twice the value of their deposits. As commission he is paid a percentage of the value of the sales by the businesses which have agreed to participate in the activities of the Club.

Before launching the Club, Denry decides to seek the patronage of the Countess of Chell in order to get the Club off to a 'right-down good starting shove'. To this end he decides to visit her at her country residence, Sneyd Hall. By accident he finds himself locked in the mansion. He tries in vain to attract the attention of someone in the Countess's employ to let him out. As he wanders from one magnificent room to another he becomes familiar with the luxury of the Countess's home. Eventually he is discovered by a housekeeper who is making her nightly rounds to ensure that the house is secure. Denry makes his escape by crashing through an enormous window, running through the park and all of the way home. The terrified housekeeper reports the event in greatly exaggerated terms, describing the burglar as a terrifying, huge man, armed with a revolver. For a period of time, Denry is fearful that he will be unmasked as the night burglar of Sneyd Hall. A reward of £20 is offered by the Earl of Chell for the capture of the intruder.

Denry's initial fears prove unfounded, however, as he turns misadventure to advantage as usual. He is urged by his tenants to set the idea of the Universal Thrift Club in operation. He has discussed the Club with all his tenants, in part trying to establish the popularity of the idea, but also to gain their approval and support. This is crucial as he intends that they should make up the core of the Club's initial membership. Convinced by the demands of so many people that the Club will prosper, he sets it up and it is an immediate success. He adds further to his reputation as a discreet and confidential friend of the Countess of Chell by writing a detailed description of the splendours of Sneyd Hall for *The Signal*. Denry's popular image as a man who succeeds – and in the popular consciousness deserves to succeed – reaches even greater heights.

COMMENTARY:
Denry sees the Universal Thrift Club as a philanthropic venture which will induce thrift in the working man. In fact – as with the modern-day universal plastic credit cards – it has the opposite effect. Under Denry's scheme the working man will be allowed to spend up to twice the amount of money he deposits. Since Denry's 'modest remuneration' comes from the businesses which participate in the Club's activities at the rate of two pence in the shilling, these businesses will encourage spending to compensate for this percentage. Denry says himself that he will show a very sizeable profit from this 'philanthropic' venture.

NOTES AND GLOSSARY:

victoria:	a low, four-wheeled carriage with a collapsible hood with seats for two people and an elevated seat in front for the driver
trap:	a two-wheeled springed carriage
sandwichman:	a person hired to carry advertising boards which are worn over the shoulders on the front and back of the body

Chapter 7

The enormous success of the Thrift Club is troublesome to Denry, as the growth in business and the number of members in the Club means that he finds himself spending all his time in tedious tasks of administration. He is an adventurer not a clerk, and so he hires Penkethman, a book-keeping genius with thirty-five years' experience, to manage his business accounts. Penkethman takes over the day-to-day administration of Denry's business affairs with great efficiency, but even so, such is the demand for the service the Club provides that Denry finds he is under-capitalised and in danger of being bankrupted. It is now more imperative than ever for Denry to enlist the patronage of the Countess of Chell. He decides that after the failure of his previous attempt to secure an audience with her, he will need to use all of his cunning and influence to create a situation in which he can present his proposal to the Countess in the most positive light. He conspires with her footman to have her carriage break down on the way to an important public engagement at the Policemen's Institute at Hanbridge and rescues her by an opportune arrival in his victoria at the scene of the accident. He then offers to take the Countess to her engagement in the victoria, and she gratefully agrees. The journey almost ends in disaster when Denry's mule races out of control through the streets of Hanbridge, intimidated by a large number of policemen (which it particularly dislikes). Denry appears to break his arm during the wild chase so that the Countess is forced to take over the reins and drive. On their arrival, the Countess is ushered inside with Denry, who is seen by one of the distinguished guests, Sir Jehosophat Dain, as an interloper and a nobody. His opinion of Denry is continually contradicted by the Countess, who praises Denry in her references to her journey and sympathises with him for accidentally breaking his arm in his hurry to get her to the reception on time. Sir Jee, as he is known, leaves the hall early, disgusted at Denry's prestigious position. This presents a dilemma, as he had been expected to second the vote of thanks to the Countess at the end of the ceremony. With typical panache, Denry solves the problem by making a brief but witty speech involving an ironic reference to the policemen assembled in the audience. This has the desired comic effect, and stands as the humorous highlight of the ceremony. Denry completes his success by taking the Countess to tea in a local tea-room, a new experience for her, but a delightful one, as she is passionately fond of tea. Here, they are able to talk privately, and as a result, the Countess, indebted to Denry for all of his chivalrous help, becomes the 'Patroness of the Universal Thrift Club'. Her support is recorded, together with photographs and a news story, in *The Signal*, and Denry is congratulated on his first appearance in the public life of the Five Towns. It now becomes possible for him to obtain as much capital as he requires at reasonable rates of interest. No one notices that his arm has not been broken. Denry has pretended that it has been broken to heighten the drama of the moment and to win the Countess's sympathy. Neither does anyone discover that the Countess's footman has suddenly acquired shares in the Thrift Club. These events prove further just how sophisticated and cunning Denry has become in his attempts to get his own way.

NOTES AND GLOSSARY:
lorgnon: an eyeglass or eyeglasses
quidnunc: an inquisitive person; a gossip. (From the Latin 'What now? What is happening?')

none so dusty: not bad going; at a good pace
mountebank: a trickster or charlatan

Chapter 8

Denry's success – he is now earning some £4000 a year – allows him to take care of his ageing mother, which he does with generosity and compassion. Mrs Machin, who is a fiercely independent woman, insists she will remain in the tiny cottage she and Denry have shared all his life. He is wealthy enough to provide a better home for her, but she resists all of his attempts to persuade her to move. Her cottage is cold; but when he buys her a sealskin shawl to ward off the cold, she puts it away for safekeeping – old habits die hard. When she then becomes ill with flu, Denry contracts it as well, and he realises that a move to a better house has become a priority. He has the sense, however, to realise that to get his mother away from her mean little cottage, he will have to use a roundabout method. He accomplishes his purpose by means of an elaborate deception. Pretending to act as the agent for a rich former Bursley resident, one Mr Wilbraham, who is acquiring property in Bursley (among it Denry's mother's), Denry coaxes his mother to visit this man's substantial new home in Bleakridge, a fashionable district of the Five Towns. Once they are there and his mother has been duly impressed by what she describes as the most sensible kind of house she has ever seen, Denry reveals that the house is in fact his own and that it is her new home. Denry has not only hoodwinked his mother with his deception, he has hoodwinked the whole town. They had believed him when he told them that he was the agent for Mr Wilbraham, when in truth Wilbraham was nothing but Denry's invention. The town does not hold this deception against Denry, as the amusement he has provided more than makes up for it, and indeed, the town rewards him by appointing him a Town Councillor.

COMMENTARY:
Denry admits in this chapter that he had not set out to be a philanthropist when he founded the Universal Thrift Club, but rather, consistent with his aim in life, 'his unique intention was to grow rich by supplying a want'. This admission puts some of his benevolent actions in a new light.

Chapter 9

Denry has retained his interest in journalism, writing the occasional article for *The Signal*. He is approached by Mr Myson, a Manchester newspaper proprietor with experience of London and the world outside Bursley. Mr Myson wants to convert his newspaper, the *Five Towns Weekly*, to the *Five Towns Daily*. He sees in Denry a man of vision, entrepreneurial skill and daring, and he seeks Denry's participation in his plan. Denry is flattered by the tribute Mr Myson pays him as an astute businessman, and invests £1500 in 'The Five Towns Newspapers, Limited'. But as soon as the new paper appears on the street, *The Signal* mounts a campaign against it by harassing its delivery boys. An attempt to hire unemployed men as an alternative delivery workforce fails because they feel it is beneath their dignity to sell newspapers. The struggle between the two newspapers gathers momentum and is in danger of becoming ugly as each side applies various techniques to sell the most papers and as *The Signal* steps up its campaign of harassment. The most notorious of these incidents is *The Signal*'s entrapment of the *Daily*'s delivery boys on the day of a crucial football match. *The Signal* offers the *Daily*'s boys toasted cheese and jam tarts and then confines them in an enclosed warehouse and its yard. With the opposition safely out of the way because it cannot deliver its newspaper, *The Signal* expects to have the market to itself on the day of one of the most important news stories of the year. Denry at last seems to have been out-witted.

Denry, though, is not to be outdone, and wins again by turning the tables on *The Signal*. He commandeers the wagons of a circus which is hired each year and which is travelling to Bursley to entertain the newsboys of *The Signal*, and uses these to carry and sell the all-important edition of the *Daily* in all parts of the Five Towns. Moreover, he has bought up all the copies of that day's issue of *The Signal*. To celebrate his victory over *The Signal* Denry organises a special Five Towns *fête* to which all members of the Thrift Club are invited. At the *fête* he reveals a new 'shy' that he has invented: a row of railway signals is set up, contestants are invited to knock down all the signals, and when they do are rewarded with a box of Turkish Delight wrapped in torn remnants of copies of *The Signal* which Denry had bought up at a halfpenny each. The contest signifies Denry's defeat of *The Signal* in the battle of the two Five Towns newspapers.

Shortly afterwards secret emissaries of *The Signal* buy shares in the *Daily* and, after negotiations with the new option holders, the *Daily* is closed down. Denry is satisfied: by playing *The Signal* at its own game, he has scored supremely – his reputation as a card is far higher than ever – and, although he is not entirely happy with the financial settlement, he has had enough of the perils of the newspaper business.

NOTES AND GLOSSARY:

Martinmas Saturday: the period of the Feast of St Martin, on 11 November

paregorical figures: Bennett is here pointing out the humour of the clown's misunderstanding of the two words 'allegorical' and 'paregoric'. The figures around Jupiter are allegorical, traditional characters from myths and legends. A paregoric is, in contrast, a particularly unpleasant medicine used to relieve diarrhoea

'Well, you're a caution': 'Well, you're a character; you're a card'

Decalogue: · another term for the Ten Commandments

Chapter 10

While Denry's fortunes continue to increase, those of Nellie Cotterill's father, Councillor Cotterill, go in the opposite direction. Denry is acquainted with the Councillor from the time he met the family in Llandudno, and Cotterill was responsible for building Denry's magnificent home, now called 'Machin House'. Despite the fact that there is a recession in the community, he has continued to build houses, for which at present there are no buyers. This has forced him to borrow increasing amounts of money in expectation of the end of the recession, and he has eventually found that he can no longer pay this money back.

Denry arrives at the Cotterills' house to show off his newly acquired motor car and is greeted with the unexpected sight of Ruth Earp, recently returned to Bursley as a widow after the death of her husband, a rich man from beyond the Five Towns. As the now free and wealthy Mrs Capron-Smith, Ruth has acquired an extra dimension of good taste in Denry's eyes. He is no longer bothered by her extravagance now that she can pay for it herself.

Councillor Cotterill arrives with the news that he is having to file for bankruptcy. Denry at last has the upper hand over a man who has patronised him for more than ten years, and a distinctly cruel side to Denry's nature appears. This is not apparent in his dealings with Mrs Cotterill, whom he likes, nor Nellie, but only against the pompous and now impecunious Councillor. Cotterill suggests that Denry might like to help him out financially, but Denry is deaf to his suggestion and responds in an unsympathetic and uncharitable way. Cotterill tells him that his brother is a thriving builder in Canada, who has offered to go into business with him. The family will now have to sell up in the Five Towns and set off for a new life in Toronto.

Ruth undertakes to help the impoverished Cotterills with their travel arrangements, and Denry expresses his sorrow that young Nellie should have to give up her life in Bursley to go to Canada. A chance remark from Nellie alerts Ruth to the shocking fact that the Councillor intends that the family should travel in steerage on the ship – the lowest class of accommodation. He intends to use the money saved by this economy to make some show of wealth to salvage his pride when they disembark in Toronto. The family have set off for Liverpool to board the boat a day early in order to book into their lowly berths. Denry is outraged and tells Ruth that he will telegraph Liverpool to get the family transferred to first class and that he will travel to Liverpool to persuade them to accept his help. Ruth offers to accompany him and to share the cost, but cautions him that a move to first class accommodation would only cause embarrass-ment, as the Cotterills no longer have clothes fine enough to allow them to dress for dinner; she suggests second class as a better alternative.

Denry telegraphs accordingly, and he and Ruth set off for Liver-pool to persuade the Cotterills to accept their offer of help. His colla-boration with Ruth on this mission of mercy makes him feel even closer to her, and he senses that this time he really will marry her.

When they get to Liverpool, Denry and Ruth stand on the promenade-deck of the liner *Titubic*, seeing the family off. They have succeeded with some effort in persuading them to transfer to second class, and this has left Mrs Cotterill in particular upset – torn between her feelings of shame and gratitude. Councillor and Mrs Cotterill go aboard, and Ruth, after saying her final goodbyes to Nellie, makes her way towards the landing stage. Denry and Nellie glance at each other as she is about to go, and in an impulsive gesture, Denry spirits her to a cab and they head for the railway station, leaving Ruth behind, lost and forgotten. Nellie is confused and anxious and asks Denry what he is doing. He surprises himself by exclaiming that he intends to marry her. He later meets Ruth at Euston station, and in reply to her enquiry as to his purpose there, he tells her that he is 'Only honeymooning'.

NOTES AND GLOSSARY:

steerage: the lowest form of accommodation on a passenger ship

'I've got the dibs': 'I've got money'

Chapter 11

Once married, Denry and Nellie travel to Switzerland on their honeymoon. Their choice of destination is no careless whim, but the result of the elegant description of the country by Ruth Capron-Smith as *the* place for the wealthy and fashionable to go. On the train from Dieppe, Denry and Nellie pretend to be bored with each other in the way that married couples come to be – or so Denry believes – all the while conscious of their unfamiliarity with the ways of their wealthy and seasoned fellow travellers. As their experience increases so does their self-confidence. One evening Denry falls into conversation with a 'thin, drawling, overbearing fellow with an eyeglass'. Denry had contracted a dislike for this man from the moment they had boarded the train. Determined to appear more wordly-wise than he is, Denry tells him that he and Nellie have been married for two years and conveys the impression that they are widely travelled and familiar with the favoured winter holiday resorts of Switzerland. When they arrive at the Hôtel Beau-Site in Mont Pridoux they 'hit it off' with all their fellow guests except a Major Clutterbuck and his family, who complain about everything and whose sole pleasure is in anticipating the arrival of their friend Captain Deverax. Believing the Hôtel Beau-Site inadequate to the needs of the Captain's impending arrival, the Clutterbucks, amid much fuss, remove to the neigh-bouring Hôtel Métropole. On the issue of the quality of the hotels, Denry and Nellie become involved in a rivalry between the guests of the two establishments. The rivalry intensifies when it is revealed upon his arrival that Captain Deverax is the 'eyeglass johnny' Denry had met on the train from Dieppe. Deverax's fearful snobbishness is more than Denry can bear. And when he learns that Denry and Nellie have only recently been married and that Denry's claims of his worldliness are specious, Deverax treats Denry with disdain and amusement. Denry, while admitting he is the author of his own embarrassment, determines to get his own back on Deverax.

Denry has established a small reputation for himself at the resort for his dexterity and bravery on the luge, a one-man toboggan. He is quite upstaged by Deverax, who shows himself proficient in the eminently fashionable art of skiing. He skis in a remarkable pair of check breeches, baggy trousers for sporting wear, attracting the awe and astonishment of the assembled smart set. His pride is somewhat tarnished, however, when Nellie, a beginner on skis, goes out of control and crashes into the Captain and the Countess Ruhl, a Russian lady whom Deverax would like to impress and to whom he was in the process of giving a skiing lesson. Nellie's ski pole takes a chunk out of the Captain's breeches, and it seems to be no little coin-cidence that after this unfortunate incident, Denry 'rewards' her by giving her an opal bracelet.

Denry decides to take his revenge in full on Deverax for his pomposity, and creates an elaborate ruse around the Captain's fondness for the Countess Ruhl. The Countess has hired a large sleigh which she uses to travel the mountain roads around the resort, sometimes accompanied by a servant, sometimes alone, but usually wearing a red cloak which makes her very easy to recognise. The Captain has been spotted on several occasions following the figure in the red cloak on the Countess's afternoon rides, which suggests that their friendship is growing ever warmer. The Hôtel Beau-Site announces that it is to hold a fancy-dress ball, and much of the talk about this event is whether the Countess and the Captain will appear together. On the afternoon of the ball, the Countess receives a telegram that necessitates her immediate departure for Russia. Denry sees her now abandoned sleigh and red cloak, and decides on his plan. He dresses as the Countess's coachman in a fur coat, and Nellie puts on the red cloak. They then set off into the thickening snow in the sleigh. Soon they find they are being followed by a figure on skis, and they lead this figure further and further out in steadily worsening conditions, before, on a particularly steep hill, the skiing figure plummets through a hedge and into a farmyard.

Back at the fancy-dress ball, Denry appears from the waist up to be dressed as a Chinese man, but from the waist down he has adopted the extravagant style of Captain Deverax. He has commissioned the tailor at Montreaux to make him a pair of breeches just like the Captain's, and he wears tight leggings and carries an eyeglass. Nellie was supposed to be dressed as Lady Jane Grey, but instead she is wearing the Countess's red cloak. Denry then carries out an accurate but fairly cruel imitation of the Captain to the general amusement of the guests, and remarks to the Clutterbuck family on the absence of the Captain and Countess. Mrs Clutterbuck asks Denry if he is implying that the Captain and the Countess have gone off together, but Denry denies that this is what he meant. Denry telephones to find out if the 'mystery skier' (who is obviously the Captain) is all right, and returns with his arm in a sling, to the confusion of the guests. He then proceeds to perform a comic routine, involving an attempt to insert his eyeglass into his left eye with his right hand.

The next day, Denry encounters the Captain, who has his arm in a sling, and who claims that he had an accident the evening before when out skiing following the Countess's sleigh. He is observed by the people at the luge run in his check breeches and his sling, exactly as Denry was dressed. General hilarity ensues, and the poor Captain, in attempting to insert his eyeglass into his left eye with his right hand to find out what the laughter is about, merely consolidates the accuracy of Denry's impersonation and increases the laughter of the growing audience at the luge run. It is then established, to the Captain's anguish, that the Countess could not have been out the night before, as she was already on her way back to Russia. The Captain therefore appears to have been chasing imaginary Countesses. Humiliated, the Captain and his friends the Clutterbucks leave the Hôtel Métropole. This means that the number of guests and the prestige of the Hôtel Beau-Site where Denry is staying is now greater than the Métropole, and so Denry has again won a total victory over the things he dislikes, both people and institutions.

NOTES AND GLOSSARY:

Plots! Nihilism! Secret Police! Marble-palaces!: this is a reference to the period of the 1905 Revolution in Russia, when there was a great deal of political activity which appeared romantic to the outside world

nemine contradicente: without contradiction

Light Brigade at Balaclava: the Charge of the Light Brigade took place in 1854 during the Crimean War (1853–6), fought by the British and French against the Russians in Turkey

Mazeppa . . . mustangs: *Mazeppa* (1819), a poem by Lord Byron, tells the story of a Polish nobleman, who, as punishment for entering into an intrigue with the wife of a local magnate, is tied naked to a horse, which is lashed and runs all the way to the Ukraine where it dies and Mazeppa is rescued by peasants

Chapter 12

Denry has conceived the ambition to become Bursley's youngest Mayor. Though there is only a faint hope that this could come about in the natural course of events, because there are two Councillors in line before him, his chances are considerably enhanced when one of these rivals dies suddenly of the 'fashionable malady of the time', appendicitis. Now he must 'upset the apple cart' of Councillor Barlow, his one remaining rival, the man who should be the next Mayor because of the number of years' service he has given to the community. Denry achieves his ambition by saving the Bursley football club from being sold by Barlow, who is the Chairman of Bursley Football Club Limited. The club has been consistently losing games and, because of low attendances, has also been losing money over a number of years. Councillor Barlow has invested a consider-able amount of his own money in an attempt to stop the club going bankrupt. Even though they recognise these facts, the citizens of Bursley are angered by the thought that they will lose their football team. Denry astounds a public meeting held in Bursley Town Hall to discuss the matter by not only suggesting that the club's problem is that it needs new talent, but by then producing England's finest footballer, Callear, and displaying him to the cheering townspeople. He explains that he has negotiated Callear's transfer to the Bursley team and that he has paid the transfer fee himself. There could not be a more popular choice, as not only is Callear a great player, but he is in fact a native of Bursley.

In his first game for his new club, Callear scores a magnificent goal in the opening minute of play. He becomes the idol of Bursley. A letter has 'appeared' in *The Signal* suggesting that because of his generosity to the football club and by extension to the town, Denry would make an ideal candidate for Mayor. A deluge of similar letters follows and several Councillors take up the call. The result is that Councillor Barlow's candidacy is shelved for a year, and Denry becomes Bursley's youngest ever Mayor, thus reaching the summit of his achievements.

Part 3

Commentary

The element of autobiography

The Card is a humorous comedy of character and circumstance, which like the best of Bennett's writing draws on his early life in the Potteries. Many critics have noted that Bennett's writing is most comfortable when he is dealing with the familiar atmosphere of the Five Towns. This has the effect of making the situations realistic and the writing assured. In this case it also allows Bennett to exploit the eccentricities and quirks of Denry and his circle for the purposes of comedy.

There are several incidents and characters in the novel which bear direct comparison with Bennett's personal experience. So far as the characters are concerned, there is obvious significance attached to the fact that Bennett gives Denry the same birth date as himself. This would appear to provide substance to the suggestion that in Denry, Bennett has created a fantasy figure with many of the attributes he was proud of in his own character, and several he would like to have had. Denry is decisive and astute in business matters, as was Bennett in his dedication to making a successful living from his writing. Denry is eccentric and perhaps even rakish in appearance, just as Bennett had a reputation as a dandy and a snappy dresser. Denry is fascinated with wealth and the 'good life', just as Bennett was. But on the other side of the coin, Denry is friendly and outgoing in manner, while Bennett was painfully shy and suffered from a severe stammer. It could also be argued that Denry's ultimate 'magnificence' portrays a level of affluence to which Bennett perpetually aspired but which, as a novelist in a declining market, he could never quite hope to attain. Of the other characters in the novel, the most convincing case for a sketch taken from personal experience is the Countess of Chell, (known affectionately in the Five Towns as 'Iris') probably modelled on the Duchess of Sutherland. Slightly less convincing is the testimony of H. K. Hales, a boyhood friend of Bennett's, who claimed to be the model for Denry and attempted to win a share of the royalties of the book, both claims which Bennett dismissed. He subsequently went on to publish a memoir entitled *The Autobiography of 'The Card'* in which he repeated his claims.

As noted in the Detailed Summaries above, a point related to Bennett's reliance on autobiographical recollections is his employment in *The Card* of a favourite device – featuring characters from his other Five Towns novels and stories. Apart from the mention of Anna Tellwright, the heroine of *Anna of the Five Towns*, characters such as Henry Mynors, Charles Fearns, Mr Duncalf and Sir Jee Dain appear in significant roles in other books.

In terms of situations, there are clear reference points for a number of events in the novel. Like Denry, Bennett was also a rent collector for a short time. The 'Great Newspaper War' (Chapter 9) is based on Bennett's recollection of the feud between the *Sentinel* newspaper and a new paper, the *Staffordshire Knot*, founded and edited by William Owen and Joseph Dawson, two of Bennett's father's friends. Bennett's father was a shareholder in the venture and eventually saw the *Knot* (mirroring the experience of the *Daily* with *The Signal* in the novel) taken over by the *Sentinel*. The episode at Llandudno and Denry's report of it for *The Signal* recalls Bennett's first piece of journalism which he began in a cardish, daring way with the word 'And'.

Characters

Denry

We cannot look at Denry as a character in the same way as we would look at characters in other novels. Unlike our estimation of traditional protagonists, based on an analysis of their actions and attributes as individuals, we must look at Denry as a portrayal of a definite type – a card. In many ways, Bennett is idealising the card in his portrayal of Denry. He is consistently eccentric and amusing, disarmingly witty and always ready with a quick retort. He is daring and opportunistic, with a capacity for kindness and a less appealing ruthless streak. From the moment when he first feels the desire to be 'truly magnificent', Bennett builds up a catalogue of success upon success in which Denry is never compromised or defeated, whatever the odds.

Clearly this is a fantastical presentation of a mythical character type, saved from being merely tiresome and ludicrous because the author never assumes to have any pretensions beyond the wish to amuse his audience. This is a point worth reiterating – *The Card* has no ambitions to be a serious novel beyond its limited story. Serious aspects emerge in passing throughout the narrative, and these are considered in the other sections of the Commentary, but they are of subsidiary importance to the general reader and are of most interest to the student wishing to understand the genesis of Bennett's comic vision. These realistic elements help to convince us of the plausibility of the situation, confirming that the good must co-exist with the bad, but they are never allowed to inhibit Denry's progress or introduce a more solemn note amongst the comedy. Denry resembles characters in Bennett's other novels in his self-reliance, resilience and indomitable spirit. In this novel it is his intention that Denry's positive qualities should outweigh and also distract from the moments when, in order to get his own way, he behaves in a ruthless and unscrupulous manner. Bennett succeeds to some extent, but the reason he is not entirely successful may have something to do with the comic purpose of the story. Denry's uncharitable behaviour, in particular in his instant reaction to Councillor Cotterill's plight, distract from the light-hearted comedy, and it is clear that Bennett was worried about this possibility. His analysis of Denry's behaviour in his meeting with the Councillor in the Cotterill house, given immediately after the exchange, is contrived and unconvincing, acting as it does as an attempt to justify an unwelcome distraction from the comedy. It also jars somewhat with other aspects of Denry's character, as although he always puts himself first, he is not averse to helping others at the same time.

Although Denry is a portrayal of a 'character type' – in some ways he is no more than a stereotype – the reader should remember that this does not affect his position as an influential figure in the novel. Unlike other novels, notably those of Dickens, in which stereotypes are relegated to secondary roles, Bennett chooses to base the entire novel around the achievements of Denry's predominant cardishness. All the other characters remain underdeveloped, as their purpose in the novel is not to create situations within which Denry acts, but, rather, to be catalysts to or recipients of Denry's ascent to magnificence. On this understanding, it is remarkable how effectively Bennett sketches some of these subsidiary characters.

Mrs Machin

Mrs Machin hardly appears in the novel, yet she is clearly a powerful influence over Denry. She is very much set in her ways and is something of a stock character, always complaining and never satisfied with her son, however successful he becomes. This is shown most clearly in Denry's attempts to get her out of the cottage he has lived in with her all of his life and into the new house he has built for her. It takes an elaborate ruse to convince her, and although she is clearly impressed by the house and all of its amenities, she eventually leaves without being asked, to return to another cottage on Brougham Street where she lived before. In this behaviour and in her suspicion of Denry's wealth, she is symbolic of the ingrained perceptions of Five Towns society which Denry undermines so successfully.

Nellie

The character of Nellie shows most clearly Bennett's skill in creating vivid life from only a few details. Nellie emerges as a sensitive girl, at first inhibited and shy like many adolescents, eventually assured and mature, without inhibitions, but keeping the girlish, somewhat naive charm which delights Denry so much. The development of their relationship is handled with great subtlety. Denry begins by treating her with superior indifference at the ball and then is guilty of ignoring her when he transfers his attentions to Ruth Earp. He is touched by her kind note thanking him for his hospitality in Llandudno, and without knowing it, this tiny gesture of affection influences his decision to marry her. In the final chapter, he is delighted with married life, realising that Nellie understands him implicitly. Notice that this assessment is seen entirely from Denry's point of view – like all of the other characters, Nellie is not allowed to express herself in any way except in relation to Denry. This factor makes it all the more impressive that Bennett manages to make Nellie a convincing character in her own right. Nellie is responsible for the most touching moment in the novel, when Mrs Machin notices the unspoken 'chemistry' between Denry and Nellie during the guided tour of Machin House, the best example of dramatic understatement in the novel and testimony to the skill Bennett was able to summon in his writing.

Ruth Earp

Ruth Earp is the most fully developed of the secondary characters in the novel, and in this she is unusual. She is also unusual in that her appearances in the novel show her to be a wholly independent woman of some means who is wilful and stands up to Denry when all others succumb. She is unsympathetically presented as a chronic spendthrift, with no understanding of economy. Denry's initial attraction to her appears to stem from his recognition and admiration of much in her character that he prides in his own. She appreciates and desires the very best that money can buy, places tremendous importance on the figure that she cuts in public, and this has the effect of making her a shallow and limited character. It is not totally clear as to why Denry decides against a second engagement, eventually reacting against his tender feelings for Ruth on the train to Liverpool. Perhaps his decision is subconsciously taken precisely because she is so like him. Denry is egotistical, and if there was a danger of Ruth outshining *the* card, he would not be able to accept it.

Councillor Cotterill

We watch the Councillor on the down slide, just as we watch Denry on the way up. Cotterill is used in the novel to emphasise the development of Denry's magnificence by acting in all ways antithetical to Denry's character. Cotterill is rude and patronising and personifies all of the middle-class vulgarity which the stylish Denry succeeds in avoiding. He is steady rather than creative and is used to comic effect as a pompous representative of shabby provincial gentility. Bennett gleefully parodies the Councillor's snobbery in his description of the Cotterill household. He is shown up in the latter stages of the book as not only an arrogant man, but a bad businessman. His relationship with Denry provides us with a serious moment of doubt about Denry's moral standing. By rejecting the Councillor's plea for help, with the narrator giving the excuse that he had been called 'young man' by him once too often, we are left with some doubts as to Denry's charitable side.

Other characters

Other characters such as the Countess of Chell, Harold Etches, Widow Hullins, Mr Myson and Sir Jee Dain are used purely as ciphers in the development of the action. The Countess, in particular, could have been further developed to show an intriguing contrast between Denry and the aristocracy, but this would have got in the way of developing the comic narrative, so she remains merely sketched in.

Structure

The Card is written in the *picaresque* tradition, a narrative form developed in Spain in the sixteenth century from the pioneering anonymous text, *La Vida de Lazarillo de Tormes* (*c.* 1554). The Spanish word picaresque means 'to do with rogues', and indeed the form is often used to catalogue the adventures of a rascal or reprobate, perhaps most famously in the works of Henry Fielding, such as *Joseph Andrews* (1742) and *Tom Jones* (1747). A picaresque work follows a biographical pattern in an episodic structure, charting the progress of the roguish protagonist from one social class to another or from one professional class to another. The form is often used for satire or social criticism. The protagonist ranges on a scale throughout works of literature from the almost evil rogue to the amusing 'character' who is mainly harmless, similar to Denry. The form has been adapted as an element of many great works of literature, not only novels. Byron's great poem *Don Juan* (1819–24) uses many of the aspects of a traditional picaresque novel for satirical and comic effect.

In *The Card*, Bennett uses this simple structure without decoration and to great effect. It is worth remembering the way in which Bennett would work on a book. *The Card* was written in under two months, and this rate of work was not at all untypical of Bennett's output. A simple structure allows the writer to concentrate on the words on each page as he writes them rather than having to cross-refer to other sections of the book at intervals. He also wrote this novel, as he noted in his journal, '. . . with a serial public very much in mind'. The episodic structure was perfect for this purpose, each chapter self-contained and easily digestible, with few serious matters of plot continuity to remember from one episode to the next apart from Denry's 'cardishness'. The success of this formula has been shown by the appearance of Chapter 1 of the novel in many anthologies of short stories under the title 'Denry at the Dance'.

Language

The language of the novel is unrelievedly plain. There are no telling turns of phrase and no distillations of experience into memorable lines. Bennett is not a quotable writer; his language is as utilitarian as his style. The sentences are almost always simple, and the range of linguistic devices such as simile and metaphor employed are few and far between.

The same plainness applies to quoted speech, especially the verbs used to introduce it. Generally, Bennett relies on 'he said', 'she demanded', 'he explained'. On occasion this is qualified for effect, to add zest or suggest complexity in the character's thoughts, such as 'he said, joyously', 'she murmured, softly', 'she exclaimed defiantly'. These are the limits to linguistic complexity, limits typical of Bennett's utilitarian written style and typical of the straightforward speech used in reality by the people of the Five Towns.

Some critics have seen this as the most significant drawback when considering Bennett's standing as a great author. This may have some bearing when considering his more serious writing but not in relation to an unpretentious entertainment such as *The Card*. As was pointed out in the section on Characters, the lack of decoration leads to a subtle quality of understatement in the best dialogue and description, most effectively exhibited in charting the development of the relationship between Denry and Nellie. Further to this, the limitations of language restrict the amount of detail in the description of landscape and scene, which means that the novel relies more heavily than most on character and dialogue. This is quite appropriate for this novel, based as it is so firmly around the actions of the central character, Denry Machin. Restricting himself to the language and idioms of the Five Towns, Bennett provides an accurate reflection of the society from which his work emerges.

Comedy and irony

The central purpose of the novel is to 'cheer up' the audience through Denry's exploits and adventures. Denry's actions are entertaining because they are original and daring, and because on the whole he acts to impress and amuse. There is an exciting feeling for the audience in watching Denry move from situation to situation on the verge of disaster, never quite falling over the edge.

In terms of characters and dialogue, humour is provided on one level by the presentation of comic stereotypes such as Mrs Machin and Councillor Cotterill. Denry makes his own contribution to this aspect by his dexterity with the witty one-line. His instant response with 'don't you?' or 'do you?' to a question from a social superior – be it the Countess of Chell, Sir Jee Dain or Councillor Cotterill – is a summarising device, used to show that Denry has got the better of the situation. This repeated line from a comic character is a very traditional comic device, used (or overused) to this day in the 'catchphrase' of the television situation comedy character. In the novel, Denry tends to overuse these catchphrases, and Bennett relies to an exaggerated extent on the comic potential of Denry uttering quaint colloquial phrases.

The most effective use of comedy in the novel is in the extended scenes of farce. The pantechnicon ride with Ruth Earp, Denry's imprisonment in Sneyd Hall, the mule ride to the opening of the Police Institute, the hijacking of *The Signal*'s anniversary parade – all of these are classic instances of farce. Again there are many parallels to the great chases in modern cinema. From the Keystone Kops in the 1920s up to the car-chase and caper movies of the 1970s, the eccentric journey filled with mishaps has amused audiences. Bennett does well to make effective use of this largely visual device in the novel, unlike his less assured attempts to use the medium of slapstick and sight gags. The laboured scene in Switzerland involving Captain Deverax, and Denry's impersonation of him is crude and unconvincing. Instead of appearing brilliant and amusing, Denry seems cruel and petty – not the author's intention at all.

Irony in the novel is restricted to the parody of the pretensions of Councillor Cotterill and the foibles of other caricatures such as Widow Hullins and Mrs Machin, although it is true that the novel is based on a fundamentally ironic assumption. Denry is able to dupe and convince everybody by sheer nerve rather than industry – an ironic comment on his society and its priorities. The ironic descriptions of Widow Hullins's house and the Cotterill house are two good examples of Bennett's command of the ironic observation.

Moral perspectives

Bennett intended the readers of the novel to respond to Denry's occasional lapses of taste and his dubious business methods with a charitable shrug and a secret smile of admiration. This is successful to some extent, but on occasion there is a danger that Denry might lose sympathy because he has gone beyond what could be called humanitarian behaviour. His treatment of the bankrupt Cotterill is not suitably explained and is the worst of his uncharitable acts. Other examples of his ruthlessness are mentioned in passing. Denry threatens the suppliers of the Thrift Club when they indicate their displeasure at having to offer Club members very favourable terms of credit. He says he will open his own co-operative stores if they do not continue to supply on the same terms, and they acquiesce because they fear that Denry would do it. This sort of coercive relationship is hardly the stuff of the jocular, self-confident card; more that of the ruthless bully. This unappealing aspect of Denry's character also emerges in his treatment of Captain Deverax, which seems to stem from envy rather than legitimate grievance. These are minor incidents, less important than the effect that Denry's ascent to 'magnificence' must have on those who do not have the luck and abilities that he has, uncomfortable factors not discussed in the novel. Though worth making, these criticisms should not distract from the fact that this is not a novel which should be taken too seriously.

Social problems

The same can be said for social problems as can be said about moral perspectives – they are alluded to at brief moments in the narrative, but are of subsidiary importance to the main themes. An example of how Bennett eschews social problems for the purposes of comedy occurs in Chapter 9, 'The Great Newspaper War':

> The state of the earthenware trade was supposed that summer to be worse than it had been since 1869, and the grumblings of the unemployed were prodigious, even seditious.

As the economy of the Five Towns depends almost entirely on the health of the Potteries, the decline in business is very serious for the unemployment situation. Denry's attempt to entice the men to take the jobs vacated by the bruised and battered newspaper boys fails because the men are too proud to be seen selling newspapers and would rather live on bread and water than do the job. This potentially important issue is immediately discarded in favour of further descriptions of comic schemes to solve the newspaper boy shortage. Such pride and inflexibility as that shown by the unemployed earthenware workers is also exhibited by Mrs Machin in her attitude to moving out of her cottage. Denry, on the other hand, stands in complete opposition to this viewpoint. He is single-minded and cunning, unlike all the other characters in the novel. Bennett may be making a social comment on the stagnation of those around Denry by presenting his actions as so entirely successful.

Part 4

Hints for study

THIS SECTION provides assistance for those studying *The Card* as an examination text. Reading a text for examination purposes is different to reading it uncritically and purely for enjoyment. A good deal of the reading we do is for the simple pleasure that reading gives us. Reading a text to prepare for an examination, on the other hand, means close and active reading of the text in order to answer such fundamental general questions about a work of literature as the following:

1) What is the author aiming to achieve through his story?
2) What does he want his readers to learn?
3) How does he go about achieving his purposes?
4) How does he use the elements of fiction – narration, description, setting, plot, point of view, character, dialogue, tone, irony, literary devices – to achieve his purposes?

Bearing these general points in mind, the most important consideration is to know the story very well. This means familiarising yourself with the details of the novel, and this comes about from successive and increasingly careful readings. You can make notes on the action of the story as you read; you can comment on characters, their natures and their actions; you can set down questions about aspects that puzzle you, with the thought of returning to consider them another time. It is very helpful when considering a novel such as *The Card* to remember these details, because the episodic nature of the narrative tends not to rely on the continuity of repeated incidents or recollections, making it more difficult to form an overview of the complete novel. By cataloguing the development of Denry's career, you can begin to see how Bennett has constructed the narrative and, through this, approach an examination question with greater assurance.

Specimen examination questions

Examination questions fall into several categories, each of which follows a standard method in dealing with the materials of a text. These categories are listed below together with examples of typical questions and answers. Answers to examination questions are short essays written under greater pressures of time than ordinary class essays. The method and approach involved in preparing an answer to an examination question, however, is the same. It requires disciplined organisation and control, and a central idea or topic sentence. It requires a set of paragraphs which show a systematic and logical development of ideas based on the topic sentence. Everything in your answer should be directly connected to the question or statement and should be aimed to convince your examiner that you fully understand the question. The answer, that is, should have unity and coherence. It is important in most cases to take time to prepare a brief plan or outline of your answer before setting it down in essay form. Determine, first of all, the topic sentence. This can often be a rephrasing of the question. In deciding on the topic sentence, other elements in the text in question will suggest themselves as evidence which you can draw on to elaborate and support your argument and ideas. What may seem to take valuable time in an examination will, in the end, save time, because preparing your outline will focus the requirements of the question for you.

Context questions

It is important to be familiar with details of the book because you may be asked context questions. These are questions in which you are asked to identify a passage from the book in order to demonstrate that you are familiar with it, understand what is being said or done and appreciate how the particular passage relates to the rest of the chapter, or the book as a whole. Only passages that are central to the main action of a book will be chosen for context questions.

Retelling of a small part

You might be asked to retell an episode or event in the novel in order to show how it relates to the general action of the book, how it advances the plot, enhances the conflict, illuminates character or reveals authorial attitudes.

Describe Denry's visit to Liverpool to see the Cotterills at the time of their departure for Canada.

Describe Denry's first visit to the Sports Club.

Retelling of selected parts

When answering a question instructing you to retell or describe certain actions or relationships in the plot of a novel, you are really being asked to show how the selected parts form an element – a theme or sub-plot – which enhances the development of the story as a whole.

Trace Denry's relationship with Ruth Earp.

What part does the Countess of Chell play in Denry's life?

Explanation of a passage

This is the simplest kind of question you will be asked – simple, provided you have mastered the details of the plot and action of the novel. Often you will be asked to offer a detailed explanation for the purpose of showing the relationship of the passage – and it will usually be a key passage – to the progress or the resolution of the story and to a revelation of the author's intention.

Explain how the Thrift Club operates.

Is Denry's greatest achievement as a 'card' the hiring of the footballer, Callear, to play for the Bursley side?

Comparison

You may be asked to compare one character with another, one relationship with another, or one incident with another.

Compare Denry and Councillor Cotterill as businessmen.

What are the chief differences between Ruth Earp and Nellie Cotterill, and why does Denry choose Nellie over Ruth?

Opinions and criticism

You may be asked to express an opinion of the book in terms of whether you like or dislike it. You may be asked to comment on the opinions of critics who have studied the book, or asked to comment on dialogue within the book, to speculate on why the author has had a character make a particular statement. Such questions usually ask you to discuss or comment on, to state whether you agree or disagree. Whatever the form of the question it supposes that you have an intimate knowledge of the text, that you have firm opinions about it and that you can support your response to the question, whether it asks for your personal opinion or for your response to the opinions of others, with evidence drawn from the text.

'And yet . . . what's he done? Has he ever done a day's work in his life? What great cause is he identified with?' Is this a fair criticism of Denry's activities? Or is the final statement in the book – 'He's

identified . . . with the great cause of cheering us all up' – a satisfactory way of summing up Denry's achievement?

Preparing an answer

Be certain before you begin to answer an examination question that you understand precisely what is asked of you. Read the question with care and take time to consider its implications. Make brief notes on the elements of the question and consider the various responses that can be made to these elements in your answer. Be careful not to answer a question that is *not* asked and to include in your answer only those points which bear directly on the question. This may seem an unnecessary caution: but often, especially when you are very familiar with the book under review, you will be tempted to show your expertise and to include extraneous material in response to a specific question.

What follows are suggestions about the information and comment which might make up answers to different kinds of examination questions. These are not samples of ideal answers. You might want to rearrange the order in which various points referring to each of the questions are set down, or you may wish to add other points that you feel ought to be taken into account when answering a question. You may wish to delete some of the materials presented below. Whatever the case, you are invited to prepare a formal response to the various questions based on the materials provided.

Context questions

> He could not comprehend why she had so laughed, save on the supposition that he was more humorous than he had suspected. Anyhow, he laughed too, and they parted laughing. He remembered that he had made a marked effect (though not one of laughter) on the tailor by quickly returning the question, 'Are you?' And his unpremeditated stroke with the Countess was similar. (Chapter 1).

You will recognise this as the scene when Denry, with great daring, asks the Countess to dance (and is probably surprised when she accepts his invitation). What is important about the scene is that Denry recognises for the first time the device or tactic through which he will eventually advance his career. He does not think that by turning the Countess's question back on her he has been particularly humorous – indeed he admits his surprise. But he recognises that in some indefinable way he has been clever, and furthermore, that in turning the question on the questioner he has seized an advantage.

He recalls that a similar tactic has worked with the tailor. This is a technique which Denry will continue to use as his career advances. You should try to recall, from your knowledge of the novel, other instances when Denry employs this tactic, or something resembling it, for the purposes of gaining an advantage, and include such references in your answer to a question. In this instance, you will recall that for his audacity Denry wins a bet of five pounds (a considerable sum of money at the turn of the century) from his rich young rival, Harold Etches. In other words, there is a reward for audacity.

Retelling of a small part

Describe Denry's visit to Liverpool to see the Cotterills at the time of their departure for Canada.
When Denry learns that the Cotterills are sailing in steerage (the cheapest kind of accommodation), from Liverpool for Canada, he decides to travel to Liverpool and to rescue them from this ignominy by paying for more suitable quarters. Ruth Earp travels with him, and it is she who saves Denry from embarrassing the Cotterills in a different way. Denry is prepared to purchase the best accommodation available, in part, perhaps, as a way of displaying his increasing affluence. Ruth Earp points out that this would be as great an embarrassment to them as travelling in steerage because they would not have the wardrobe and other resources commensurate with the affluence that first-class travel implies. Denry takes the point and makes suitable arrangements. He then recognises that Nellie will make a more suitable mate than Ruth and spirits her away from the vessel before it sails. There seems little doubt that Denry takes the action he does as much to display his wealth and flaunt his good fortune in relation to the destitute Councillor Cotterill, as he does to ease their journey. You may think of other instances of Denry's philanthropy which in fact disguise the more serious purpose of advancing his career.

Describe Denry's first visit to the Sports Club.
The temptation in a simple question such as this one would be to relate what happens before and after the first visit Denry makes to the Sports Club, to examine his aspirations and the way in which he was invited to become a member. Bennett uses Denry's first visit to the Club in order to show that this is another social hurdle which he must overcome in his rise to magnificence. Denry, timid and uncertain, finds himself alone, apart from the Club's chief steward, and takes the opportunity to conduct a reconnaissance of the

institution, emphasising his satisfaction at joining this particular elite. It is only then that he comes into contact with other Club members.

Retelling of selected parts

When asked to describe a particular part of a novel – either a scene or the actions of a certain character or characters – you should be able to present a précis of that particular scene of action as directly and concisely as possible. You should also know the novel well enough to be able to comment on how this particular scene or action elaborates the development of the story or the characters who are principals in it.

Trace Denry's relationship with Ruth Earp.
Denry first meets Ruth Earp when he goes to her for dancing lessons in anticipation of attending the civic ball. She is offhand with him both when teaching him and at the ball. He next encounters her when he attempts to collect rent in arrears from her on behalf of a client. He discovers she is quite cunning in attempting to escape Bursley without paying her rent, by making various promises which he finds out she does not plan to keep. He rescues her from the runaway pantechnicon and develops an interest in her which results in their engagement. His illusions about her are shattered when he travels with her (and her chaperone Nellie) on a summer holiday and realises that she is a reckless spendthrift. He decides that her problem is incurable and breaks off the engagement.

Ruth reappears in the Cotterills' home as a rich widow, and Denry is impressed with her increased style and subtlety. As they travel in first-class comfort to Liverpool, he contemplates a renewal of their former engagement, something which it appears Ruth would find acceptable. In a sudden, and unaccountable – if perhaps typical – reversal of form, Denry abandons Ruth for Nellie, Councillor Cotterill's daughter. Bennett's point, though we must infer this from the text, is that perhaps Ruth is too like Denry, an alter ego, and that she would compromise him in some way, or attract equal attention, taking the limelight away from him if they were to marry. What is more apparent is that there seems to be no genuine affection on Denry's part for Ruth Earp. He seems more attracted by superficial considerations – her glamour, his covetousness, her sophisticated manner. His relations with her have nothing to do with affairs of the heart. The same might be said of his marriage to Nellie. They seem perfectly at ease with each other, but nothing more than a simple fondness between them is evident. Each conspires to keep their recent wedding from being known by those around them in

Switzerland, even though they are on their honeymoon. This kind of presentation of character is not typical of Bennett who, in his serious writing, is masterful in portraying the widest range of emotion. You might speculate on why this is so, keeping in mind Bennett's purpose in writing the novel and its relation to the picaresque tradition.

What part does the Countess of Chell play in Denry's life?
The Countess of Chell figures in three events in Denry's life, all of which substantially advance his fortunes. The first (as we have observed) is at the civic ball when, by laughing at his remark on the dance floor and again when leaving the ball, the Countess conveys the impression – or at least those citizens of Bursley present infer – that there is a special intimacy between herself and Denry.

The second occasion is when Denry visits the Countess's stately home with the hope of inducing her to become a patron for his Thrift Club. He misses seeing her, is confined for some time in Sneyd Hall, makes his escape without being identified, fears for a time he will be found out and, when things settle down, writes a long and detailed description of the house which further enhances the popular belief that he is on intimate terms with the Countess.

The third occasion is when Denry contrives with a footman to have the Countess's carriage break down on her way to an important public occasion in Bursley. He rescues her, gets her to the appointment on time, and shares the public platform with her. This is his first appearance in the public affairs of the community, and attracts more attention than it might normally because he is with the Countess. Impressed by Denry's gallantry, which she does not realise is contrived, the Countess agrees to become the patron of the Thrift Club. The success of this scheme means that public confidence in the Club is restored and Denry is saved from financial embarrassment.

Explanation of a passage

Explain how the Thrift Club operates.
Denry creates the Thrift Club to act as an intermediary between consumers and the local traders of Bursley. For a guaranteed weekly investment from patrons, Denry issues credit of up to double the value which can immediately be spent. His profit comes from the shopkeepers and merchants who participate in the scheme: they give Denry a percentage of the money spent on goods purchased, as payment for the service he provides. The scheme succeeds too well: so popular is the credit plan that people subscribe in numbers greater than Denry could have anticipated, and thus there is a severe drain on his limited capital. Because of this, and because of the inherent

conservatism of the banking institutions of Denry's day, he finds it difficult to arrange for the bridging finance which will tide him over periods of heavy spending. He eventually solves this problem by winning the patronage of the Countess of Chell. Once he has the support of the Countess, the Club prospers and provides the basis of Denry's fortunes.

Is Denry's greatest achievement as a 'card' the hiring of the footballer, Callear, to play for the Bursley side?
Denry has built his reputation on being a 'card', doing the unexpected through acts of daring that others can only think about. The people of the Five Towns get vicarious pleasure out of Denry's constant inventiveness and, because they come to see Denry as someone special, in some way superior to themselves, they do not resent his successes. Denry does possess the instinct to get to the heart of a situation, to see what is most important in it so far as his own personal interests are concerned. Time and again, an act of public benefaction is really motivated by pure self-interest. The case of getting Callear signed up as a member of the Bursley football team epitomises Denry's curious genius. The equation is a simple one: Denry wishes to be Mayor; his rival for the office of Mayor is Chairman of the board of the Bursley Football Club. The club is losing money; the rival to Denry, having tried in an honourable way to save the club, to the extent of putting in a good deal of his own money, announces that the club must close down. Denry buys Callear, a Bursley native and England's best footballer. Thus Denry performs his greatest feat as a 'card' – he is seen to be the most generous of men because he has appealed to the thing that matters almost as much as life itself to an Englishman of the working classes, a successful football club.

Comparison

Compare Denry and Councillor Cotterill as businessmen.
Denry succeeds in business because he has an awareness of what will appeal to the majority of people, a sense of how to market his ideas and a reputation for being successful which, once it is established, causes people to believe he will succeed further. Because of this they support him. Denry's motives may at times be dubious but his methods are always just within the law. He understands, for example, that holidaymakers are all susceptible to new kinds of entertainment, and he is quick to exploit the wreck of the Norwegian ship at Llandudno, by buying the lifeboat on which to conduct tours, by marketing the lemon chocolate as a cure for seasickness, and by

entering into partnership with the local photographer to provide mementoes of the vacation to those who want them. Similarly, he anticipates modern credit financiers in developing the idea of the Thrift Club, and once it is launched, in hiring a first-rate accountant to look after its affairs. Denry, as he says of himself, is a man of ideas with very shrewd notions of what sorts of enterprises will succeed. As we see, he often turns what he thinks of as certain failure into gain, and he always professes surprise at how successful he is in his endeavours.

We know much less of Councillor Cotterill's financial affairs than we do of Denry's. He, like the other characters in the novel, is a foil to Denry, presented by Bennett to heighten his dramatisation of Denry's success. We do know that Councillor Cotterill is a bad judge of his business market. He is a builder, and he seems not to be able to tell good times when people can afford to have houses built and bad times when they cannot. He seems not to be able to learn from his experiences nor, despite his bankruptcy, understand the full extent of his failure. It is his folly and stupidity in managing his affairs so badly (when his problems were essentially simple ones and easily comprehended) that causes Denry to treat him with contempt rather than sympathy.

What are the chief differences between Ruth Earp and Nellie Cotterill, and why does Denry choose Nellie over Ruth?
Ruth Earp and Nellie Cotterill are opposites in temperament and character. They, too, are foils to Denry, intended to expose aspects of his character. Ruth is the more fully developed, perhaps because she is not sweet and simple like Nellie. Like Denry, Ruth is opportunistic and self-interested; any act of benevolence is incidental to what she achieves from committing it. She applies whatever means seem most likely to protect or advance her interests, and she reveals a range of emotions – snobbishness, artistic talent, financial conniving, coquettishness, among others – to win favour. Perhaps because he recognises these qualities in Ruth and sees them as similar to his own, Denry in the end does not marry her.

Ruth is more interesting than Nellie because almost perfect goodness of heart, which Nellie possesses, is less interestingly displayed in fiction than is its opposite. Nellie is a flat character, a person of simple goodness. When Denry conceives his idea of becoming the youngest of all Bursley's Mayors, she is compliant and ready to perform the duties of a Mayoress. But Nellie remains a very minor figure in the story.

Opinions and criticism

'And yet . . . what's he done? Has he ever done a day's work in his life? What great cause is he identified with?' Is this a fair criticism of Denry's activities? Or is the final statement in the book – 'He's identified . . . with the great cause of cheering us all up' – a satisfactory way of summing up Denry's achievement?

It might be perfectly fair to say that the book is devoted to 'cheering us all up' and nothing more, as the final anonymous speaker in the novel claims, especially when we consider Bennett's own view of the book: he regarded it as a trifle, aimed to entertain a mass reading market through serial publication. That it was taken more seriously than he intended is indicated by his surprise at how popular and successful the book was when it appeared, and by how popular it has remained ever since.

The job of the critic is to discuss the author's intention and to comment on his success in achieving his goals. But it is more than that, involving an attempt to detect meaning beyond that originally planned by the author. In light of this objective, finding answers to the questions posed by Councillor Barlow at the end of the book is an important job of the critic. There is no doubt that Denry is satisfied with the reputation he gains through his daring behaviour. Further, there is no doubt that he is at pains to protect that reputation – he wants to be the 'very ace in the deck'. His various activities are aimed at increasing his material well-being, and while he may never have done an honest day's physical labour in his life, he expends a good deal of mental energy to ensure his success. The luck that accompanies his deeds is no more than that of any other successful person engaged in similar potentially dangerous financial schemes.

We must remember as well that Bennett had a profound understanding of the community he was writing about and the aims and values of that community. Denry is more than amusing; he is admired because he has, through his own ingenuity, risen above his initial station in life – from lawyer's clerk he becomes Mayor of the town. Not only has he forged success out of modest beginnings, he remains in the town, and this is greatly to his credit. In achieving success, Denry makes life more enjoyable for his fellow townspeople than it might otherwise have been, not only by making people laugh, but, in material terms, by creating the Thrift Club, through his ingenious manipulation of banking practices. So in a distinct sense, each of the comments summing up Denry's reputation is valid: they go together to describe the whole man.

Part 5

Suggestions for further reading

The text

The Card, Penguin Twentieth Century Classics, Penguin, Harmondsworth, 1991.

General reading

BARKER, DUDLEY: *Writer By Trade: A View of Arnold Bennett*, Allen and Unwin, London, 1966.

DRABBLE, MARGARET: *Arnold Bennett: A Biography*, Weidenfeld and Nicolson, London, 1974.

HEPBURN, JAMES G.: *The Art of Arnold Bennett*, Indiana University Press, Bloomington, 1963.

LUCAS, JOHN: *Arnold Bennett; A Study of His Fiction*, Methuen & Co., London, 1974.

POUND, REGINALD: *Arnold Bennett: A Biography*, William Heinemann, London, 1952.

WEST, REBECCA: *Arnold Bennett Himself*, The John Day Co., New York, 1931.

WOOLF, VIRGINIA: 'Modern Fiction' in *The Common Reader*, Harcourt Brace and Co., New York, 1925.

YOUNG, KENNETH: *Arnold Bennett*, Longman, Harlow, 1975.

The author of these notes

G. D. KILLAM was educated at the University of British Columbia and London University and spent a number of years in Africa – at Fourah Bay College, Sierra Leone, the Universities of Ibadan and Lagos in Nigeria and the University of Dar es Salaam. He has worked for a number of years in Cameroon with colleagues on a programme in education for self-reliance. He has written studies of the writings of Achebe and Ngugi and is the editor of *East and Central African Writing in English*. For twelve years he was editor of *World Literature in English*.

York Handbooks: list of titles

YORK HANDBOOKS form a companion series to York Notes and are designed to meet the wider needs of students of English and related fields. Each volume is a compact study of a given subject area, written by an authority with experience in communicating the essential ideas to students at all levels.